PATTERNS, ROUNDS

— AND —

JOYFUL SOUNDS

Melodies and Accompaniments to Energize Rehearsals and Performances

ARRANGED BY
JOHN LEAVITT

To access digital PDF files, go to:
www.halleonard.com/mylibrary

Enter Code
8600-7521-3942-8460

HAL•LEONARD®
CORPORATION
7777 W. BLUEMOUND RD. P.O. BOX 13819 MILWAUKEE, WI 53213

Visit Hal Leonard Online at
www.halleonard.com

In Australia Contact:
Hal Leonard Australia Pty, Ltd.
4 Lentara Court
Cheltenham, Victoria, 3192 Australia
Email: ausadmin@halleonard.com.au

About This Book

The tunes in this collection are delightful music. When these melodies are sung as rounds, they produce harmony as a wonderful by-product. Rounds are a great way to introduce and teach young ears the concept of harmony.

I have found that with a little creativity, these short tunes, 8-12 bars in length, may be enlarged to engaging music that can grow to 2-3 minute presentations. I'm always looking for ways to "tune my singers' ears" even at the collegiate level. These tunes can be fun for all ages.

About the Ostinato Patterns

I have written ostinatos or patterns to accompany the rounds in this collection. I have used a two-octave set of tone bells, but handbells and/or Orff instruments can work just as well (see below). Some of the directions in the ostinato parts are as follows:

- **LV** = Let vibrate; in other words do not dampen the tone over rests.

- **Staccato dots** over the notes indicate that the player should dampen the ringing tone of the bell so that the tone bells have a more percussive effect. This is accomplished by having the player place the index finger on the side of the vibrating portion of the bell.

Additional octaves and pitches can be used in these patterns if you have a larger set of tone bells. Handbells can easily be substituted or added for additional color. The staccato dots for handbells would also indicate that the player should dampen the ringing tone of the bell. This is accomplished by placing the thumb on the base of the bell.

Orff instruments may also be substituted effectively. For the ostinato parts marked LV, these should be played by a metallophone if possible. The ostinato parts with staccato dots should be played by a xylophone.

Teaching and Performing the Ostinatos and Rounds

Teach the Ostinato pattern, which is usually a three or four-bar pattern. Have the ensemble sing the tune with each ostinato part. Build the pattern by pyramiding or stacking the next part on top of the previous part.

Start the song by pyramiding or stacking the ostinato instrumental patterns. As the patterns continue, have the ensemble sing the melody in unison, followed by singing the melody in a round.

When the round is completed have all instrumental parts play one more full time. The ostinato pattern then "deconstructs" by Part 3 concluding at the end of its pattern, followed by Part 2 concluding at the end of its pattern, followed by Part 1 concluding at the end of its pattern. Note that Part 1 should end on the downbeat on a final tonic (key) note.

About the Digital Files

We have included a PDF file of each of the rounds and ostinato patterns that can be downloaded and projected or printed. Enter the code in the inside front cover of this book at **www.halleonard.com/mylibrary** to download the files.

Have Fun!

John Leavitt

1. Alleluia

Traditional
Arranged by John Leavitt

Pronunciation and Translation:

Alleluia
Ah-leh-loo-jah

Praise the Lord

Teaching Suggestions:

1. Teach this simple Latin word, making sure to use tall vowels without diphthongs.

2. Teach the tune in two separate four-bar phrases. Note the leaps in the first phrase and the steps in the second phrase.

3. Practice the melody as a round in two groups.

4. Teach each part of the ostinato. Have the ensemble sing with each part. (See front notes for instructions on stacking.)

5. Start the song by pyramiding or stacking the ostinato pattern. As the pattern continues, have the ensemble sing the melody in unison, followed by singing the melody in a round.

    Option: sing repetitions in unison or in a round using terraced dynamics (soft-medium-loud).

6. When the round is completed, "deconstruct" the ostinato. (See front notes for instructions on deconstructing.) Note that Part 1 should end on the downbeat on a final C long note rather than the G, ie C-G-C.

OSTINATO PATTERNS

REHEARSAL NOTES

2. Cherries So Ripe

This fun tune is an Old English street cry. Street cries were short musical calls of merchants selling their products and services in open-air markets.

Teaching Suggestions:

1. Teach the vocal part in two-measure phrases.

2. Sing the four phrases sequentially.

3. Sing the melody as a round in two-parts, three-parts, and/or four parts.

4. Experiment with terraced dynamics (soft-medium-loud) making each two measure phrase a little louder.

5. Teach each part of the ostinato. Have the ensemble sing with each part. (See front notes for instructions on stacking.)

6. Start the song by pyramiding or stacking the ostinato pattern. As the pattern continues, have the ensemble first sing the melody in unison, followed by a two, three, or four part round. You may choose to have the ensemble continue by singing each new entrance of the melody at a different dynamic level. When the round is completed, "deconstruct" the ostinato. (See front notes for instructions on "deconstructing.")

OSTINATO PATTERNS

♩ = ca. 112

Part 1

Part 2

Part 3 & 4 (Or Part 3 on metallophone)

REHEARSAL NOTES

3. Christmas is Coming

Traditional English Folk Carol
Arranged by John Leavitt

Christ - mas is com - ing the goose is get - ting fat,

Please to put a pen - ny in the old man's___ hat,

Please to put a pen - ny in the old man's hat.

Teaching Suggestions:

1. Teach the vocal part in four-measure phrases.

2. Sing all three phrases sequentially.

3. Sing the melody as a round in two-parts and/or three-parts.

4. Teach each part of the ostinato. Have the ensemble sing with each part. (See front notes for instructions on stacking.)

5. Start the song by pyramiding or stacking the ostinato pattern. As the pattern continues, have the ensemble first sing the melody in unison, followed by a three-part round.

6. Have the ensemble sing the melody in unison at a "f" or loud level. Sing a repeat of the melody in unison at a "p" or soft level for contrast.

7. Follow with the ensemble singing the three-part round twice also with these dynamic contrasts.

8. When the round is completed, "deconstruct" the ostinato. (See front notes for instructions on "deconstructing.")

OSTINATO PATTERNS

REHEARSAL NOTES

4. Da Pacem Domine

Melchior Franck (1573-1639)
Arranged by John Leavitt

Pronunciation and Translation:

Da pacem, Domine
Dah, Pah-cehm, Daw-mee-neh
Lord, grant us peace in these our days.

Teaching Suggestions:

1. Teach the Latin words in rhythm, echo style. Be sure to use tall vowels without diphthongs.

2. Teach the vocal part in two-measure phrases.

3. Sing all three phrases sequentially.

4. Sing the melody as a two-part round. (1 & 2)

5. Teach each part of the ostinato. Have the ensemble sing with each part. (See front notes for instructions on stacking.)

6. Start the song by pyramiding or stacking the ostinato pattern. As the pattern continues, have the ensemble first sing the melody in unison, followed by a two-part round. You may choose to have the ensemble contrast repetitions with terraced dynamics (soft-medium-loud). When the round is completed, "deconstruct" the ostinato. (See front notes for instructions on "deconstructing.") In the final four bars of Part 1, the last measure should end with the lower G in Part 1.

7. For a greater challenge, you may sing this round as a canon at the 5th. In other words, teach vocal parts 1 & 2 as written. Teach vocal parts (3) and (4) the same melody starting on D as a tonic. When ready to build your canon, use the following order: Part 1 starts (on G), Part 3 follows on beat 3 (on D), Part 2 starts in the 2nd measure on beat 3 (on G) and Part 4 starts in the 2nd measure 3 on beat 1 (on D).

OSTINATO PATTERNS

REHEARSAL NOTES

5. Derrie Ding, Ding, Dasson

Thomas Ravenscroft (c. 1582-1635)
Arranged by John Leavitt

Thomas Ravenscroft was an English composer who lived at the end of the Renaissance. He is best known for his collections of rounds and part songs.

Teaching Suggestions:

1. Teach the vocal part in four-measure phrases.

2. Sing the three phrases sequentially.

3. Sing the melody as a round in two-parts and then in three-parts.

4. Experiment with terraced dynamics (loud-medium-soft).

5. Teach each part of the ostinato. Have the ensemble sing with each part. (See front notes for instructions on stacking.)

6. Start the song by pyramiding or stacking the ostinato pattern. As the pattern continues, have the ensemble first sing the melody in unison, followed by a two and/or three-part round using terraced dynamics.

7. When the round is completed, "deconstruct" the ostinato. (See front notes for instructions on "deconstructing.")

OSTINATO PATTERNS

♩ = ca. 138

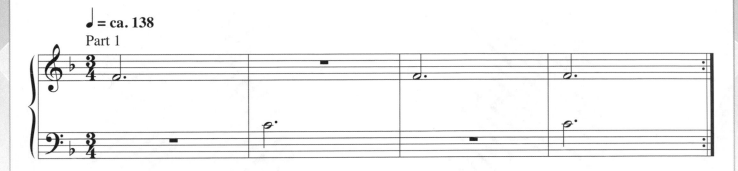

REHEARSAL NOTES

6. Early to Bed and Early to Rise

School Round Book of 1852
Words attributed to Benjamin Franklin
Arranged by John Leavitt

♩ = ca. 120

1. Ear - ly to bed and ear - ly to rise,

2. Makes a man health - y and wealth - y and wise,

3. Wise, health - y and wealth - y.

Teaching Suggestions:

1. Teach the vocal part in four-measure phrases.

2. Sing the three phrases sequentially.
   Option: teach the music first on a nonsense syllable (loo-loo), then add the words.

3. Sing the melody as a round in two parts and then in three parts.

4. Experiment with terraced dynamics (soft-medium-loud).

5. Teach each part of the ostinato. Have the ensemble sing with each part alternating between a nonsense syllable and the words. (See front notes for instructions on stacking.)

6. Start the song by pyramiding or stacking the ostinato pattern. As the pattern continues, have the ensemble first sing the melody in unison on nonsense syllables (loo-loo) then the words. Continue with a two and/or three-part round alternating each new entrance of the melody between nonsense syllables and the words.

7. When the round is completed, "deconstruct" the ostinato. (See front notes for instructions on "deconstructing.")

OSTINATO PATTERNS

$\quad \bullet$ = ca. 120

REHEARSAL NOTES

7. Ev'ning Still

Teaching Suggestions:

1. Teach the vocal part in four-measure phrases.

2. Sing the three phrases sequentially.

3. Sing the melody as a round in two-parts and then in three-parts.

4. Experiment using terraced dynamics (soft-medium) both on each new entrance of the melody.

5. Teach each part of the ostinato. Have the ensemble sing with each part.
    Option: alternate humming or singing the melody on an "oo" vowel with singing the words. (See front notes for instructions on stacking.)

6. Start the song by pyramiding or stacking the ostinato pattern. As the pattern continues, have the ensemble first sing the melody in unison, followed by a two and three-part round. Be sure to add your dynamic contrasts. Add an extra repetition of the round by humming or singing the melody on an "oo" vowel.

7. When the round is completed, "deconstruct" the ostinato. (See front notes for instructions on "deconstructing.") In the final 4 bars of Part 1, the last measure should end with a "tonic C."

OSTINATO PATTERNS

♩ = ca. 112

Part 1

Part 2

Part 3 & 4

REHEARSAL NOTES

_____

_____

_____

_____

_____

_____

_____

_____

_____

_____

8. Frére Jacques (Are You Sleeping)

Traditional French
Arranged by John Leavitt

♩ = ca. 67

1 Fré - re Jac - ques, Fré - re Jac - ques, Dor - mez vous? dor - mez vous? **2**
Are you sleep - ing? Are you sleep - ing? Broth - er John, Broth - er John,

3 Son - nez les ma - tin - es, son - nez les ma - tin - es, Din, don, din, din, don, din. **4**
Morn - ing bells are ring - ing, Morn - ing bells are ring - ing, Ding, ding, dong, ding, ding, dong.

Teaching Suggestions:

1. Teach the French words in rhythm, echo style. Teach two bars at a time. Go back and add previous phrases(s) to the one you're teaching.

   Variation: speak and tap the rhythms with your fingers.

2. Teach/sing the melody in French. Use #1 as a guide to introduce the melody.

3. Teach/sing the melody in English.

4. Sing the melody as a round in two, three, and four parts. Alternate between French and English words.

5. Teach each part of the ostinato. Have the ensemble sing with each part. (See front notes for instructions on stacking.)

6. Start the song by pyramiding or stacking the ostinato pattern. As the pattern continues, have the ensemble sing the melody in unison in French followed by English. Have the ensemble sing the melody in a round in French followed by English.
   Option: Add repetitions of the unison melody and round with terraced dynamic contrasts (soft-medium-loud).

7. When the round is completed, "deconstruct" the ostinato. (See front notes for instructions on "deconstructing.") In the final four bars of Part 1, the last measure should end on the downbeat with a "tonic F."

OSTINATO PATTERNS

♩ = ca. 67

Part 1

Part 2

Part 3 & 4

LV

REHEARSAL NOTES

9. Hashivenu

Israeli Folk Song
Arranged by John Leavitt

This text comes from the Bible, Lamentations 5: 21.

Pronunciation and Translation

Hashivenu Adonai elecha.
   Hah-shee-veh-noo Ah doh-nahee eh-leh-chah.
   (Cause us to return, O Lord, to you.)

Venashuva.
   Veh-nah-shoo-vah.
   (And we shall return.)

Chadesh yameinu kekedem.
   Chah-dehsh yah-meh-noo keh-keh-dehm.
   (Renew our days as of old.)

Teaching Suggestions:

1. Teach the Hebrew words speaking in the rhythm of the tune.

2. Teach the vocal part in four-measure phrases.
    Option: teach the music first on a nonsense syllable (la-la), then add the words.

3. Sing all three phrases sequentially.

4. Sing the melody as a round in two-parts and then in three-parts.

5. Teach each part of the ostinato. Have the ensemble sing with each part, alternating between nonsense syllables and the words. (See front notes for instructions on stacking.)

(LV this measure)

6. Start the song by pyramiding or stacking the ostinato pattern. As the pattern continues, have the ensemble first sing the melody in unison, followed by a three-part round. Have the ensemble sing the melody in unison at a "f" or loud level.

7. Sing a repeat of the melody in unison at a "p" or soft level for contrast.

8. Follow with the ensemble singing the three-part round twice also with these dynamic contrasts.

9. When the round is completed, "deconstruct" the ostinato. (See front notes for instructions on "deconstructing.") In the final 4 bars of Part 1, the last measure should end with a "tonic C."

REHEARSAL NOTES

10. Hava Nashira

Israeli Folk Song
Arranged by John Leavitt

♩ = ca. 88

1

Ha - va na - shi - ra, shir Hal - le - lu - jah.

2

Ha - va na - shi - ra, shir Hal - le - lu - jah.

3

Ha - va na - shi - ra, shir Hal - le - lu - jah.

Pronunciation and Translation:

Hava nashira, shir Hallelujah.
Hah-vah nah-sheer-a, sheer Hah-leh-loo-jah.
Come let us sing, sing praise to the Lord.

Teaching Suggestions:

1. Teach the Hebrew words speaking in the rhythm of the tune.

2. Teach the vocal part in four-measure phrases.
    Option: teach the music first on a nonsense syllable (la-la), then add the words.

3. Sing all three phrases sequentially.

4. Sing the melody as a round in two-parts and then in three-parts.

5. Teach each part of the ostinato. Have the ensemble sing with each part, alternating between a nonsense syllable and the words. (See front notes for instructions on stacking.)

6. Start the song by pyramiding or stacking the ostinato pattern. As the pattern continues, have the ensemble first sing the melody in unison at "p" or soft dynamic level, followed by a three-part round sung at a medium or loud dynamic level.

7. After the round has concluded, you may choose to sing the melody in unison one final time at a soft dynamic level, or you may "deconstruct" the ostinato. (See front notes for instructions on "deconstructing.") In the final four bars of Part 1, the last measure should end with a "tonic B♭."

OSTINATO PATTERNS

♩ = ca. 88

REHEARSAL NOTES

11. I Love the Mountains

Teaching Suggestions:

1. Teach the vocal part in two-measure phrases.
   Option: teach the melody on a nonsense syllable (la-la, loo, loo).
   Option: teach the melody and reinforce the rhythm by tapping fingers at the same time.

2. Sing the four phrases sequentially.

3. Sing the melody as a round in two-parts, three-parts, and/or four parts.

4. Experiment using terraced dynamics (soft-medium-loud) on each new entrance of the melody.

5. Teach each part of the ostinato. Have the ensemble sing with each part, alternating between a nonsense syllable and the words. Tap fingers to reinforce the rhythm and keep it crisp! (See front notes for instructions on stacking.)

6. Start the song by pyramiding or stacking the ostinato pattern. As the pattern continues, have the ensemble first sing the melody in unison on nonsense syllables (la-la, loo-loo) then the words. Have the ensemble continue with a two and/or three/four part round. Be sure to add dynamic contrasts.

7. When the round is completed, "deconstruct" the ostinato. (See front notes for instructions on "deconstructing.") After the final 4 bars of Part 1, conclude with a final strike on "tonic E."

OSTINATO PATTERNS

REHEARSAL NOTES

12. Jubilate Deo

Words from Psalm 65
Music by Michael Praetorious (1571-1621)
Arranged by John Leavitt

Pronunciation and Translation:

Jubilate Deo, Alleluia!

Joo-bee-lah-teh Deh-aw, Ah-leh-loo-jah!

(Rejoice in God, praise the Lord!)

Teaching Suggestions:

1. Teach the Latin words in rhythm, echo style. Be sure to use tall vowels without diphthongs.

2. Teach the vocal part in two-measure phrases.

3. Sing all three phrases sequentially.

4. Sing the melody as a three-part round. (parts with *)
    Option: Sing melody up to a six-part round.

5. Teach each part of the ostinato. Have the ensemble sing with each part. (See front notes for instructions on stacking.)

6. Start the song by pyramiding or stacking the ostinato pattern. As the pattern continues, have the ensemble first sing the melody in unison, followed by a round repeated in up to six parts. Use terraced dynamics (soft-medium-loud) for repetitions of the round.

7. When the round is completed, "deconstruct" the ostinato. (See front notes for instructions on "deconstructing.") When Part 1 finishes, add a final tonic "C."

OSTINATO PATTERNS

REHEARSAL NOTES

13. La Cloche (The Clock)

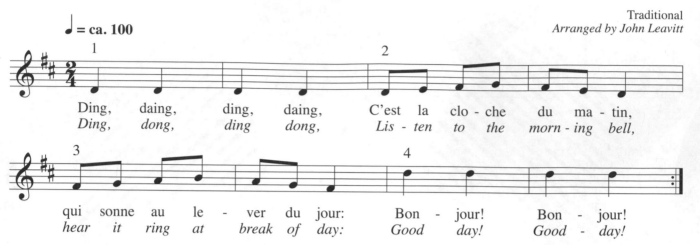

Traditional
Arranged by John Leavitt

♩ = ca. 100

Ding, daing, ding, daing, C'est la clo - che du ma - tin,
Ding, dong, ding dong, Lis - ten to the morn - ing bell,

qui sonne au le - ver du jour: Bon - jour! Bon - jour!
hear it ring at break of day: Good day! Good - day!

Teaching Suggestions:

1. Teach the French words in rhythm, echo style. Teach two bars at a time. Go back and add previous phrases(s) to the one you're teaching.

   Variation: speak and clap the rhythms.

2. Teach/sing the melody in French. Use #1 as a guide to introduce the melody.

3. Teach/sing the melody in English.

4. Practice the melody as a round in two, three, and/or four parts, French followed by English.

5. Teach each part of the ostinato. Have the ensemble sing with each part, alternating between French and English words. (See front notes for instructions on stacking.)

6. Start the song by pyramiding or stacking the ostinato pattern. As the pattern continues, sing the melody in unison in French followed by English, then sing the melody in a round, French followed by English.

7. When the round is completed, "deconstruct" the ostinato. (See front notes for instructions on "deconstructing.") In the final four bars of Part 1, the last measure should end on the downbeat with a "tonic D."

OSTINATO PATTERNS

REHEARSAL NOTES

14. Mozart Alleluia

From *Exsultate, Jubilate*, alt.
W.A. Mozart, (1756-1791)
Adapted & Arranged by John Leavitt

♩ = ca. 116

1

Al - le -lu - ia, al - le - lu - ia,____ al - le - lu - ia, al - le - lu - ia.

2

Al - le -lu - ia, al - le - lu - ia,____ al - le - lu - ia, al - le - lu - ia.

3

Al - le - lu - ia, al - le - lu - ia.

Teaching Suggestions:

1. Teach this simple Latin word which means "Praise the Lord." Be sure to use tall vowels without diphthongs. *Ah-leh-loo-jah.*

2. Teach the vocal part in four-measure phrases.

3. Sing all three phrases sequentially.

4. Sing the melody as a round in two-parts and then in three-parts.

5. Teach each part of the ostinato. Have the ensemble sing with each part. (See front notes for instructions on stacking.)

6. Start the song by pyramiding or stacking the ostinato pattern. As the pattern continues, have the ensemble first sing the melody in unison at a soft level, followed by a two-part round at a medium level, and then a three-part round at a loud level.

7. After the round concludes with the final part, have all ostinato parts finish with one more repetition as a satisfying Coda or ending.

OSTINATO PATTERNS

REHEARSAL NOTES

15. Music Alone Shall Live

German
Arranged by John Leavitt

♩ = ca. 128

1
All things shall per - ish from un - der the sky,

2
Mu - sic a - lone shall live, Mu - sic a - lone shall live,

3
Mu - sic a - lone shall live, Nev - er to die.

Teaching Suggestions:

1. Teach the vocal part in four-measure phrases.

2. Sing the three phrases sequentially.
   Option: teach the music first on a nonsense syllable (la-la), then add the words.

3. Sing the melody as a round in two-parts and then in three-parts.

4. Experiment with terraced dynamics (soft-medium-loud) on each new entrance of the melody.

5. Teach each part of the ostinato. Have the ensemble sing with each part, alternating between a nonsense syllable and the words. (See front notes for instructions on stacking.)

6. Start the song by pyramiding or stacking the ostinato pattern. As the pattern continues, have the ensemble first sing the melody in unison on nonsense syllables (la-la) then the words. Continue with a two and/or three-part round alternating each new entrance of the melody between nonsense syllables and the words.

7. When the round is completed, "deconstruct" the ostinato. (See front notes for instructions on "deconstructing.")

OSTINATO PATTERNS

♩ = ca. 128

Part 1

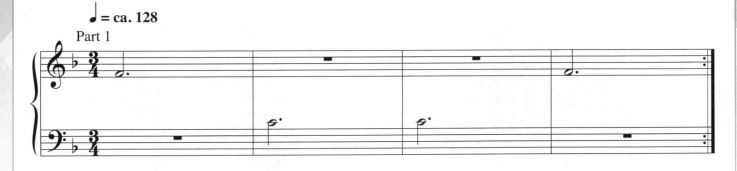

Part 2

Part 3

REHEARSAL NOTES

16. Oh, How Lovely Is the Evening

Traditional
Arranged by John Leavitt

Teaching Suggestions:

1. Teach the vocal part in three-measure phrases.

2. Sing the three phrases sequentially.

3. Sing the melody as a round in two-parts and then in three-parts.

4. Experiment using terraced dynamics (soft-medium-loud) on each new entrance of the melody. Another use of terraced dynamics would be to "echo" or sing softer the third measure of each phrase.

5. Teach each part of the ostinato. Have the ensemble sing with each part. (See front notes for instructions on stacking.)

6. Start the song by pyramiding or stacking the ostinato pattern. As the pattern continues, have the ensemble first sing the melody in unison, followed by a two and three-part round. Be sure to add your dynamic contrasts.

7. When the round is completed, "deconstruct" the ostinato. (See front notes for instructions on "deconstructing.") In the final 3 bars of Part 1, the last measure should end with a "tonic D."

OSTINATO PATTERNS

♩. = ca. 56

Part 1

Part 2

Part 3

(on repeat)

Part 4

REHEARSAL NOTES

17. One Bottle of Pop

Traditional
Arranged by John Leavitt

One bot-tle of pop, two bot-tles of pop, three bot-tles of pop, four bot-tles of pop,

five bot-tles of pop six bot-tles of pop, sev-en bot-tles of pop.

Don't put your trash in my back yard, my back yard, my back yard,

don't put your trash in my back yard, my back yard's full.

Fish and chips and vin - e - gar, vin - e - gar, vin - e - gar,

fish and chips and vin - e - gar, pep-per pep-per pep-per pop! Click*

*tongue click and/or finger snap

OSTINATO PATTERNS

♩. = ca. 56

Part 1 & Part 2

Part 3

Part 4 & Part 5

Teaching Suggestions:

1. Teach the vocal part in four-measure phrases.

2. Sing the three phrases sequentially.

3. Sing the melody as a round in two-parts and then in three-parts.

4. Experiment using terraced dynamics (soft-loud) on each new entrance of the melody.

5. Teach each part of the ostinato. Have the ensemble sing with each part. (See front notes for instructions on stacking.)

   Option: Have half of the ensemble tap their toe on each strong beat (dotted quarter note) and have the other half tap fingers on the weak beats (eighth notes on 2-3 and 5-6).

6. Start the song by pyramiding or stacking the ostinato pattern. As the pattern continues, have the ensemble first sing the melody in unison, followed by a two and three-part round. Be sure to add dynamic contrasts. Add another repetition of the three-part round and add tap toes/fingers.

7. When the round is completed, "deconstruct" the ostinato. (See front notes for instructions on "deconstructing.")

18. One May Begin

ROUND

Traditional
Arranged by John Leavitt

♩ = ca. 72

One may be - gin, then num - ber two makes a sound, num - ber

three joins in to sing a round.

Teaching Suggestions:

1. Teach the vocal part in four-measure phrases.

2. Sing the two phrases sequentially.

3. Sing the melody as a round in two, three, and/or four parts.

4. Experiment with terraced dynamics (soft-medium-loud) and even arch-shaped cresc./dim. with the melody "peaking" at the beginning of measure five.

5. Teach each part of the ostinato. Have the ensemble sing with each part. (See front notes for instructions on stacking.)

6. Start the song by pyramiding or stacking the ostinato pattern. As the pattern continues, have the ensemble first sing the melody in unison, followed by a two, three, or four part round. You may choose to have the ensemble continue by singing the melody in unison at "p" or soft dynamic level.

7. When the round is completed, "deconstruct" the ostinato. (See front notes for instructions on "deconstructing.") In the final four bars of Part 1, the last measure should end with a "tonic G."

OSTINATO PATTERNS

REHEARSAL NOTES

19. Row, Row, Row Your Boat

ROUND

Traditional
Arranged by John Leavitt

Teaching Suggestions:

1. Teach the vocal part in four-measure phrases. Encourage good diction with the use of the articulators, *the teeth, lips, and tongue.*

2. Sing the two phrases sequentially.

3. Sing the melody as a round in two, three, and/or four parts.

4. Experiment with terraced dynamics (loud-medium-soft) giving the illusion that the "boat" is traveling away in the distance.

5. Teach each part of the ostinato. Have the ensemble sing with each part. (See front notes for instructions on stacking.)

6. Start the song by pyramiding or stacking the ostinato pattern. As the pattern continues, have the ensemble first sing the melody in unison, followed by a two, three, or four part round. Have the ensemble sing each new entrance with a softer dynamic, "painting" the illusion of the boat traveling away.

7. When the round is completed, "deconstruct" the ostinato. (See front notes for instructions on "deconstructing.") In the final 4 bars of Part 1, the third measure of the pattern should repeat to end on "tonic C's."

OSTINATO PATTERNS

REHEARSAL NOTES

20. Shalom Chaverim (Shalom Friends)

Traditional Hebrew
Arranged by John Leavitt

♩ = ca. 96

Sha - lom cha - ve - rim, shal - lom cha - ve - rim, sha -
Sha - lom my___ friends, sha - lom my___ friends sha -

lom, sha - lom, Le - hit - ra - ot, le -
lom, sha - lom. We'll see you a - gain, we'll

hit - ra - ot, sha - lom, sha - lom.
see you a - gain sha - lom, sha - lom.

Pronunciation and Translation:

Shalom chaverim, lehitraot shalom.

Shah-lohm chah-veh-reem, leh-heet-rah-oht.

(The word "shalom" is a Hebrew greeting meaning "peace.")

Teaching Suggestions:

1. Teach the Hebrew words speaking in the rhythm of the tune.

2. Teach the tune in unison in Hebrew. (You can add dynamics later, this verse mf or f.)

3. Teach the tune in unison in English. (You can add dynamics later, this verse p.)

4. Have the ensemble sing both verses back to back Hebrew, followed by English.
   (Don't forget to add dynamic contrasts.)

5. Have the ensemble sing both verses back to back in a three-part round.
   (Don't forget to add dynamic contrasts.)

6. Teach each part of the ostinato. Have the ensemble sing with each part. (See front notes for instructions on stacking.)

7. Start the song by pyramiding or stacking the ostinato pattern. As the pattern continues, have the ensemble sing the melody in unison, both verses back to back, Hebrew followed by English. The ensemble continues by singing both verses back to back in a round.

8. When the round is completed, "deconstruct" the ostinato. (See front notes for instructions on "deconstructing.") Note that Part 1 should end on a final D long note rather than the A, ie D-A-D.

OSTINATO PATTERNS

REHEARSAL NOTES

21. Sing a Joyful Song

Teaching Suggestions:

1. Teach the vocal part in four-measure phrases.

    Option: in phrase 3, have the ensemble lightly clap two eighth notes where the quarter rests appear to keep a steady tempo.

2. Sing all three phrases sequentially.

3. Sing the melody as a round in two-parts and then in three-parts.

4. Teach each part of the ostinato. Have the ensemble sing with each part. (See front notes for instructions on stacking.)

    Option: alternate between the two verses.

5. Start the song by pyramiding or stacking the ostinato pattern. As the pattern continues, have the ensemble first sing the melody in unison on the first verse followed by the second verse of all fa la la's.

    Use dynamic contrasts such as having the ensemble sing in unison "f" or loud dynamic level on the first verse, followed by "p" or soft dynamic level on the second verse. Sing the round in a similar dynamic manner.

6. When the round is completed, "deconstruct" the ostinato. (See front notes for instructions on "deconstructing.")

OSTINATO PATTERNS

REHEARSAL NOTES

22. Sing Psallite

ROUND

Thomas Tallis, c. 1505-1523
Lyrics & Arrangement by John Leavitt

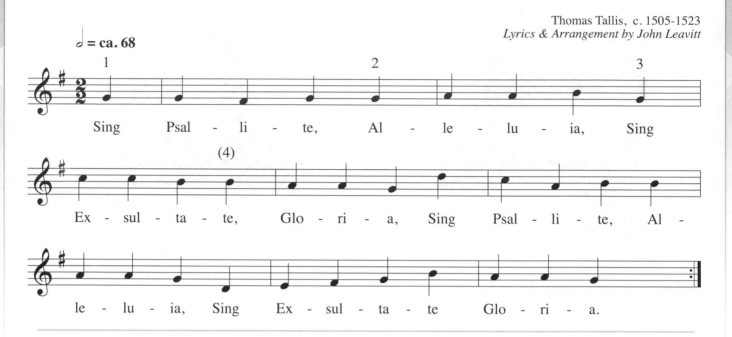

Thomas Tallis is considered one of England's greatest composers and lived during the Renaissance Period.

Pronunciation and Translation:

Psallite, Alleluia, Exsultate, Gloria.

Sah-lee-teh, Ah-leh-loo-jah, Ex-sool-tah-teh, Glaw-ree-ah

(Sing, Praise, Rejoice, Glory (to God))

Teaching Suggestions:

1. Teach the Latin words and be sure to use tall vowels without diphthongs.

2. Teach the vocal part in two-measure phrases.

3. Sing all four phrases sequentially.

4. Sing the melody as a round in two, three, and/or four parts.

5. Teach each part of the ostinato. Have the ensemble sing with each part. (See front notes for instructions on stacking.)

   Option: alternate singing between hum/oo and the words.

6. Start the song by pyramiding or stacking the ostinato pattern. As the pattern continues, have the ensemble first sing the melody in unison, followed by a two, three, and/or four part round. You may choose to have the ensemble continue by singing the melody in unison at "p" or soft dynamic level.

7. When the round is completed, "deconstruct" the ostinato. (See front notes for instructions on "deconstructing.")

OSTINATO PATTERNS

$\mathbf{\frac{1}{2}}$ = ca. 68

Part 1

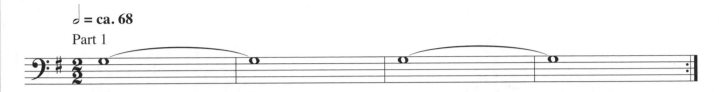

Part 2
(on repeat)

LV

Part 3

LV

REHEARSAL NOTES

23. The Bell Doth Toll

Traditional
Arranged by John Leavitt

The bell doth toll, its ech - oes roll, I know its sound full well, I love its ring-ing, for it calls to sing-ing, with its bim, bim, bim, bom, bell, Bim, bom, bim, bom, bell.

Teaching Suggestions:

1. Teach the vocal part in four-measure phrases.
   Option: in phrase three, have the ensemble tap quarter notes to keep a steady tempo.
   Option: have the ensemble close to the voiced consonant on "bim" and "bom."

2. Sing all three phrases sequentially.

3. Sing the melody as a round in two-parts and then in three-parts.

4. Teach each part of the ostinato. Have the ensemble sing with each part. (See front notes for instructions on stacking.)
   Option: alternate singing between hum/oo and the words.

5. Start the song by pyramiding or stacking the ostinato pattern. As the pattern continues, have the ensemble first sing the melody in unison, followed by a three-part round. Experiment repeating the round with dynamic contrasts to extend its length.

6. When the round is completed, "deconstruct" the ostinato. (See front notes for instructions on "deconstructing.")

OSTINATO PATTERNS

REHEARSAL NOTES

_____

_____

_____

_____

_____

_____

_____

24. The Crane

Traditional
Arranged by John Leavitt

This is a fun tongue twister and a great piece to work on the articulators: the teeth, the lips, and the tongue.

Teaching Suggestions:

1. Teach the text slowly at first, speaking in the rhythm of the melody. Work articulators for several repetitions of each two-bar phrase.

2. Teach the tune in four separate two-bar phrases.

3. Sing the melody as a round in two, three, and/or four parts.

4. Teach each part of the ostinato. Have the ensemble sing with each part. (See front notes for instructions on stacking.)
   Option: alternate between the words and the fa-la-la's.

5. Start the song by pyramiding or stacking the ostinato pattern. As the pattern continues, have the ensemble sing the melody in unison (both verses) followed by singing the melody in a round (both verses).

   Option: contrast repetitions in unison or in a round by using terraced dynamics (soft-medium-loud). End by gradually removing each ostinato part in reverse.

6. When the round is completed, "deconstruct" the ostinato. (See front notes for instructions on "deconstructing.") In the final four bars of Part 1, the last measure should end on the downbeat with a "tonic G."

OSTINATO PATTERNS

♩ = ca. 72

REHEARSAL NOTES